First Printing: February 2016
Second Printing: March 2018
Third Printing: May 2019

Printed in the United States of America

First Edition: February 2016

ISBN-13:   978-0692653807
ISBN-10:   0692653805

Third Edition

Table of Contents

About Me

I am beyond thrilled to have this opportunity to share some short stories that are loosely based on my experiences and those of others I know. During the last few years, I have spent much time reflecting on my life and how I have evolved into a strong, passionate, and purpose-driven woman. The process has been challenging and filled with periods of uncertainty, confusion, and hopelessness; many of you can relate.

In my darkest days, I sought comfort through writing and listening to music. This book will merge my love for both while creating a narrative that I hope will touch your life and inspire you to achieve greatness. Before we take that journey, let me share a little more about me, Danielle Boose-McDowell!

> I am the Founder, Resident in Counseling, and Life Coach of The Healing Space, an agency providing mental health, personal, and professional development skills to youth and young adults in the Hampton Roads VA community. I started the company to create positive changes in the lives of young people. As a youth, I was considered an "at risk" teen: I was a teen mom at age 17, repeatedly witnessed my father's substance abuse issues and grew up in a low-income household. As a result, I struggled and failed repeatedly to create a positive life for myself and my family. Many years passed before I successfully developed the necessary skills to become a healthy, productive community leader.
>
> The Healing Space's mission is to support youth and young adults with successfully

transitioning from feeling stuck to feeling empowered. The organization achieves its mission through mental health counseling, coaching, workshops and mentorship. I offer local "Life & Lyric" therapy workshops providing participants the opportunity to tackle difficult life issues through using music and writing prompts to uncover solutions and develop healthy coping skills for handling stress. To learn more, please contact me at danielleboose@gmail.com

That's enough about me; let's move onto **Life & Lyrics**!

The Legal Stuff

When the vision for this book first came to me, I thought about what had been significant along my journey and the answer was music. Throughout my life, music has always been there for me: soulful music relaxed me, hip-hop raised my consciousness (or helped me get through a workout) and gospel music reminded me that God would get me through my darkest moments.

Think about your life so far: what song have you heard that directly aligns with your experience? What lyrics seem to speak directly to your current or past experiences? Can you remember that one song that instantly takes you back to the precise moment when you knew your relationship was over? All of these attest to the power of music to ignite so many feelings as well as lead to personal growth.

In my life, music has always been along for the ride and this book will highlight some of the songs that directly align with my life and the lives of those I love. Due to legal restrictions, I will only provide the song title and artist name; however, I encourage you to take the time to listen to each song to fully understand the related story.

Referencing any song in no way implies ownership of any creative rights to said song. My objective is only to inspire you to incorporate music in your life and seek similar tools to empower you to live authentically.

Now, as promised, I present to you **Life & Lyrics: Through Danielle's Eyes** . . .

Keep Ya Head Up
By Tupac Shakur

Same drama, different day! I spent most of my pregnancy alone, without your support. You said you would be *different* but you were no different than my father. They all leave. What makes the love you had for me any different from the love all those other guys have for the women they leave to figure it out on their own?

I have been through so much and I am only 17: from the pervert who thought he'd turn me into a woman before my time to my father's repeated "vacations" to jail. Add my mother's ridiculous work schedule and you can imagine why I felt constantly alone. Now I have this little girl, who looks just like me, who will need me to be things that I just can't be. My life seems to be a constant state of hurt, stress and confusion; what's the purpose of it? How can I make life better for my daughter? I regret creating her in chaos but she has brought about a hope that I once believed would never return. Now I must figure out how to make things different for her.

As I look into her perfect eyes, smell her new baby scent and caress her soft skin, I fear that my limitations will create devastation for her. Her parents are two broken children who lack the ability and knowledge to nurture her into wholeness; I lack the ability to fill my own foundational holes. Yet I accept my limitations and I am determined to move past this darkness and find light through my love for her.

Her father may not be along for the journey but I will do everything in my power to change her life and improve her odds. God, please grant me the strength and courage to be the mother she deserves. By the way, can you straighten out her father too?

Cry
By Lyfe Jennings

Two years have passed but I'm still having nightmares; it feels like just yesterday my life was falling apart. Everyone seems to think I should just snap out of it and move on with my life as if nothing ever happened. Well Sherlock, if it was that easy, don't you think I would have been the first in line to regain happiness, safety and security?

I've been trying to play the strong one and assure my mother that everything is *just fine* but I am far from *fine*. *Fine* hasn't visited me in years and, inside, I'm full of sorrow and despair. I lost me and now I am nowhere to be found. The loss has shaken me to my core and, although you mean well, I am tired of hearing "just pray and trust God"!

I just wanna cry: cry and release all the pain. I don't want to be told that *crying won't do me any good* and I should *just let it go*. I just wanna cry: cry until there are no more tears; cry until my spirit feels the need to cry no more.

For now, I give myself permission to not be strong; permission to accept the weakness and despair. Truthfully there is nothing wrong with crying; if anyone says they are that strong, they are lying. Life has thrown me obstacles no teenager should ever have to face and suggesting that I should compartmentalize my pain or just *get over it* is pure crap!

I'm not sure if this pain will ever heal or if those images will leave my brain. Every time I hear that song by Blackstreet, my worst nightmare resurfaces and there is nothing I can do about it! In that moment, sheer terror captivates my soul and I'm not sure that I will ever be free. As the tears flow down my face, I hear my grandmother's voice reminding me, "Baby, God won't put more on you than you can bear". I cry as I pray for this strength that she says I must possess.

Your Gonna Need Me
By Dionne Warwick

It's not you, it's me: "If I were older and more established, you'd make the perfect wife." Exactly what the heck does that mean? This was a discussion we should've had before I gave you my heart including visions of two kids, a dog and the white picket fence. How could I be so naive to believe that you wanted the same thing?

I have invested so much into making this relationship work: you were different and we connected on a spiritual level (or so I thought). This BS about you needing more time is a bogus excuse to leave me. So do you and leave already! Am I bitter? Heck yeah! Am I angry? Darn right! I am angrier with myself because I should've known better. This isn't the first time my heart has been broken or that I've bet on someone that is incapable of loving me or being what I need him to be.

Well Mr. Heartbreak, I'll accept that you want to leave because I refuse to be one of those begging, pleading chicks holding on when there's nothing left to hold onto. Our connection was one-sided; a fairy tale that was merely make believe.

As our story reaches its end, your enormous scent that once filled the room decreases, I am left with memories of warm embraces and soft kisses that required me to stand on my tippy toes to reach your lips. At last we have reached our final goodbye.

But I guarantee you one thing: you're gonna want me back one day!

This Can't Be Life
By Jay-Z

Was I born to live like this? There's no way that I was brought into this world to simply exist. To spend days busting my butt to gain an education so I can secure a basic job and raise basic kids who go onto struggle through the same cycle of basic normalcy. I will not accept this as my reality; this cannot be life. There has to be something more to life than what I'm experiencing now.

I was brought here for a reason or a specific purpose; although I'm not so sure what it is, I know what it is not. I am not going to spend the rest of my life robbing Peter to pay Paul. I refuse to suffer through years of college only to be left with tons of debt to receive a low paying, unfulfilled position to work during the best years of my life. How can I look my daughter in the eye and tell her that her dreams and desires are important when I'm dedicated to a life that diminishes my own?

As I lay in bed, I envision the life I yearn to have; a life filled with new opportunities to boldly share my talents, to spark excitement and change in others and create a legacy that with dedication all things are possible. Instead, I lay here with a textbook in front of me while my stomach growls from hunger saying, "Danielle, you have to push on! Your message is bigger than you. Your sacrifices will not be in vain".

One day, the life I envision will be my reality. The heartaches, sadness and difficult times will propel me and my physical and emotional hunger will push me to greatness.

Although my current experiences seem to be doomed and I'm far from where I want to be, I'm thankful that I have the desire to pursue more and the bold stance to never accept that life is about simply existing. I will never live merely to exist!

U.N.I.T.Y.
By Queen Latifah

Oh... I'm feeling myself today! You know what I mean? When you wake up and everything seems to be going your way. I picked out my fly outfit, accessories, and even put a few curls in my hair. If you knew me, you would know this had to be birthed from today's feeling: I'm such a ponytail-and-go kind of girl.

As I walked out the door, my neighbor complimented me on my outfit, which confirmed that I was killing it today. Today was one of those days where I felt so beautiful and the happiness showed all over my face. I was en route to hang with the bestie and we were going to own the day without a care in the world. We were committed to a day of laughter, fun and memories! Wouldn't you know that, as Murphy's Law would have it, one dude would come along and *eff* it all up?

I was cute too; rocking high heels that were thankfully comfortable on my flat feet. The few extra inches provided a perfect silhouette of my figure and allowed my dress to lay perfectly against my frame. We heard the cat calls as we walked across campus but we were skillful at ignoring them. We were rude about it and didn't care; we were lost in our laughter and conversation about our plans for the day.

Then that one idiot, who apparently felt disrespected by our ignoring his "hey baby" and "hey you", proceeded to spew out all kinds of venomous statements. "You uppity b----", "You bigheaded h—"; the insults continued. He proceeded to follow us up and down the street, laughing with his ignorant friends, believing his words would diminish our beauty. The closer he came to entering our personal space, the more I was inclined to address his hateful remarks.

My bestie looked me in the eye for some kind of direction on how to proceed. I was determined that this guy wouldn't take away my feeling; the immense beauty I felt at the dawning of the day. I turned around, looked him dead in the eye and said: "U.N.I.T.Y; love a black girl from infinity to infinity!" We busted out in laughter and simply walked away. I can still see the look of confusion on his face as we walked away, singing the chorus of the song, continuing on our journey.

A Song For Mama
By Boyz II Men

I look into the light skinned woman's eyes and I see my future self. You see, this woman created me and passed on her beauty, intelligence, style, and grace. This woman, who I'm thankful to call mother, has made countless sacrifices to ensure that she raised me to be independent and God fearing. She spent her youthful years working diligently to provide me love and I am forever thankful for the person she helped cultivate.

Our relationship hasn't always been sunshine and roses: boy did we have our tough times! I remember those years when I felt she didn't care or understand me; she went from being my superhero to public enemy number one. When I reached my teenage years, I was a know-it-all and convinced that my mother was clueless. She tried with all her might to connect to me; I pushed her away, yearning for my independence and freedom. Oh how often do I wish I could turn back the hands of time and embrace those precious years! Mom would warn me, "Slow down baby; don't rush to grow up. You have the rest of your life to be grown". I followed the footsteps of many others and found out the hard way.

As the years have gone by, our relationship has evolved and we've found a space of appreciation for one another. Now that I am a mother, our past struggles have resurfaced in my daughter, giving me an all new respect for my mother. Each day I reverence her a little more because I know firsthand the commitment she made to nurture and support her children. I am dedicated to spending the rest of our time together showing her through my actions that her sacrifices were not in vain. The bond we have will continue to stand the test of time.

My mother continues to lead through her character and, even though we still bump heads from time to time, I couldn't go a day without her. Momma, I love you!

Sallie Mae Back
By Dee-1

Go to college, get a good education and then you'll have a better life. This was the message that I heard since elementary school. During my years of primary education, the word *college* became synonymous with *a better life*. Most of the advice was well-intentioned and my formal education provided an out and opportunity for higher paying jobs.

But let's be real: the debt that I accumulated along the way was ridiculous! Please don't start with the *you didn't have to use loans, there were other options* speech; I'm over it! By the time I reached college, I was a single parent with limited skills to secure high paying positions. I also lived in a small city, which further reduced my chances of financial wealth without a formal education.

So I did what many well-intentioned people do: I took out student loans. These loans provided the necessary resources to cover the ridiculously high costs of school while barely providing a roof over my head and food in my belly. (I admit, I had some wasteful spending habits that increased my debt, but that's a story for another day.) Back to these darn student loans . . .

I finished college and started my teaching career in a nearby high school. Life was good: the checks were coming, which meant financial stability, and the good life had begun (or so I thought). In a short amount of time, I received calls alerting me that it was time to payback my student loans. I looked at my household expenses and my loan repayment amount. So, you mean to tell me, I worked hard to earn my degree and to secure a "good job" and I still can't afford to maintain my expenses and pay Sallie Mae back? Are you kidding me? I have been tricked! I spent my childhood assuming a college education equated wealth when, in reality, it ADDED more debt. Now I have to figure out how to pay Sallie Mae back and manage to LIVE.

He Has His Hands On You
By Marvin Sapp

Lord, I know that you have ordered my steps: although I can't understand why I'm going through so much, I realize that it is all for your greater purpose. I am sitting here in my car, homeless and defeated but trusting that my journey is bigger than I could ever imagine. I was led to this moment in time to be reminded that, no matter how difficult and challenging life may become, you will always have your hands on me. You will protect me, heal me and comfort me when loneliness enters my spirit. God, despite the circumstance, you always remind me that you are right there.

I don't know whether it is pride or stubbornness but I refuse to pack up and go home. I refuse to allow my dreams to die. I know that, despite what the devil does, you have promised me peace and joy. I may have no home to call my own but I have faith that you will get me out of this car and prepare angels to go before me to assist me in the next stages of my journey. I pray that you will watch over me and give me discernment to know when your angels have arrived.

I left my children behind to prepare a better life for them here and my sacrifice will not be in vain. For I know that you are a God who answers prayers; I pray that you guide me, encourage me and strengthen me as I push through any obstacle that arises. Help me, oh Lord, to take this experience and bless another person; to recall the humility I've felt from being homeless and seeking shelter in my car so that I will forever be grateful of the future blessings that have been predestined for me.

I ask that you take all the wrongs of my life and make them right so I can be the mother my children deserve and a faithful servant according to your will. Watch over me Lord as I rest my eyes and keep the demons away for another night. Amen.

Daddy
By Beyonce

We've shared an unfiltered relationship for many years: I have always felt comfortable sharing all the uncomfortable things with you. I knew that no matter what I shared with you, you'd love me and give me nonjudgmental advice. There were points in my life where I felt so invaluable and you reassured me that I was worthy despite the mistakes that I had made.

You recently told me how proud you are of the woman I've become. Well Daddy, I am a representation of you: I am bold and walk in my unfiltered truth because of you. You showed me that we are perfect in our imperfections; that we have struggles as well as the strength to overcome them. You have continually been knocked down by life but you always resurface with an unwavering dedication. We've had so many fun memories: from the messy truck rides through the mud to the long walks, conversations, and times you let me step all over your feet while teaching me how to slow dance—do you remember that?

Your unconventional parenting helped me to seek out answers, make mistakes and learn from them. During my childhood, I recall missing you in your absences but never thinking for one moment that you didn't love me. You got caught up in some of the same struggles many black men in our country face today, but you refused to allow it to keep you from being a father. You have always been committed to being a better father, an amazing grandfather and, more importantly, my friend. Daddy, I thank you!

There is no one in the world who could take your place. You have shown me that love has no limitations and, as parents, we can only do the very best we can. You may not realize it but your dedication has never gone unnoticed. I am proud to be a daddy's girl and I am praying for additional countless years of laughter and love.

I'm In Love With Another Man
By Jazmine Sullivan

You're staring at me with sadness overflowing from those brown eyes. You yearn to be my knight and shining armor but I'm in love with another man. We continue to stay miserable together because we've dedicated years to making our relationship work. Neither one of us is willing to accept that the love we once had is long gone. You want to relive a past love but my heart belongs to another.

He's not the man you are, and God knows we fuss and fight, but I love him. No matter how much I try to fight the feelings and stay to make you happy, my heart yearns for another. Staying in misery would cause more damage than leaving, so let's call it quits before our love turns into hate. I am so sorry for bowing out before our happily ever after was fulfilled but someone out there will fill the void and give you what your heart desires. She will love you the way you deserve to be loved; why deprive yourself of that?

I wish I could answer your questions:

>"What does he do that I don't do?"

>"Why are your throwing away all these years?"

>"How can we make it work?"

The truth is that I don't know; I've spent months trying to dismiss my feelings and find the space in my heart that you once had. I am not naive to think that love is that lustful feeling gained in new relationships. We've had our ups and downs for years but I never imagined we'd reach an end to what we thought would be a life-long love.

I've accepted that staying in this relationship will do us both more harm than good. One day you'll look back and be grateful for our final goodbye. Your happily-ever-after woman will enter your life and give you all that your heart desires. She will be what you wanted me to be and love you in ways you deserve. I'm not sure what life has in store for me but I'm taking a gamble on the man I love.

Back In The Day
By Ahmad Lewis

I'm tired of sitting in the house so I guess I'll jump on my bike and ride out to see what my friends are doing. As the breeze blows through my hair, I head down the hill towards my home girl's house. We have been friends since I first moved to Early St and she helped to make this move better because I hated it here. Mom said living here would be better than College Hill but, so far, all of it sucks.

The move caused me to leave behind my friends and go to another school. The house is big but now it's hot as heck in the summer and cold as crap in the winter. The kids here have mostly developed friendships from years passed so I have to get in where I fit in. Thankfully, this one chick is pretty cool; we like some of the same music and her parents are pretty cool. She lives with her mom and dad, which is pretty unique to see these days. They are older than my mom but real chill and my mom is cool with me stopping by and playing with her. (Not to mention her mom has all the good snacks.)

We hang out for a while, talking about our plans for the weekend and what new things took place at school. She and I sit on the porch, watching the boys play in the parking lot across from her house. My twin is home, doing school work; she can be so boring sometimes. I am so excited to have a friend to hang with and show me around Rivermont.

I've met some of her friends and they seem pretty cool too. While we listen to music on the radio, her brother runs inside the house, yelling for her assistance. She runs inside to get whatever he wants, when I see my

24

crush go towards the parking lot. I try to act like I'm not watching him and focus on adjusting the radio. He isn't paying attention so I glance up and see him and his friends in laughter. When my home girl returns, I tell her to look at them over there. When she turns her head to look at them, he looks our way! I try to be cool but the butterflies return. I like him and I'm not even sure why I do. Something about him intrigues me but I'm not ready to let anyone know. For now, I'll hang with my friend and try to make this new place home.

Ex-Factor
By Lauryn Hill

We've been battling since the beginning of our relationship (or at least it feels that way). I spend so much time reassuring you that I care for you as much as you care for me. Who am I kidding? I'm too damn young to love anyone. If the truth be told, I don't even love myself but I don't want this young love to end because it is my first love. I've shared secrets with you that I've never told a living soul.

You've hurt me and I've hurt you too. You were my crutch and my excuse for staying is that I figured no one could be there for me like you have been. This connection isn't healthy for either of us but the uncertainty of life without you is too much to handle. I hate change and I want to stay in misery because I have embraced it.

I need you to be more than you're capable of; I need you to pour your all into me and fill the voids. The void that appeared when my father left; when his being locked up blocked him from providing the fatherly love that I so desperately need. I sought out security in you, not realizing that you're young too; you can't fix me and we can't fix us. This crazy thing we call a relationship is simply a feeling that two young people are holding onto for dear life. A feeling that once seemed like true love but it just isn't working. I walk away, you don't let me; you walk away, I beg you to return.

Every letter you've written me is scattered across my bed: I reflect on the promises we made as if we were adults. The countless phone conversations about our future and life after school. The car rides in your old car before you upgraded: you couldn't tell me that we weren't grown. The truth is, we are still children with separate paths in life that we must now take. In our hearts we know it's time to say goodbye but neither one of us is ready to walk away.

Alright
By Kendrick Lamar

Another black person killed. Another life that has gone too soon. More marches, more speeches. I'm tired of the news stories that diminish the injustices we face due to the color of our skin. The justice system continues to show no justice in *these* cases.

I hear about Tamir Rice, Trayvon Martin, Oscar Grant, Sandra Bland and all these other lives who lost the opportunity to live long enough to reach my age and I all I can feel is rage. I cried in the beginning but now I am numb to the news; when I see RIP in my newsfeed, I assume who has been murdered. What a sad state: when you've seen so many lives taken that you expect another loss.

Kendrick plays in the background while my siblings and I share our disgust for the state of our country. When will things be different? Will my son grow up to face many of the same injustices? How do I explain to my son that sometimes people will mistreat you solely because of the color of your skin?

The challenge is that, despite having an African American President, we are disproportionally incarcerated, in poverty and have the highest rates of health concerns. Regardless of all the strides we have made and our continued fight to overcome the obstacles, we are forced to live with the awareness that our lives or freedom can be taken away at any time.

Some say that we have no reason to demand the lives of our race matters because ALL lives matter. Well if ALL lives mattered, the racial injustices we face would cease to exist and there would be no need for a movement to address them. I have faith that we will be alright and I will do my part to be a change advocate so my son will grow up without the war stories of yesteryear. I will continue to fight because I refuse to accept this future for my children. I'll fight through my voice, I'll fight through empowering others, I'll fight through supporting those who continue to sacrifice their lives and demand that Black Lives Matter!

Just Another Day
By Queen Latifah

The music is loud from the car stereos: you can hear the bass from the speakers before the car enters our street. Young kids are out playing in the street, there's laughter in the air and periodically you smell traces of weed from some neighborhood teens sneaking to smoke behind the bushes.

When I say I'm from Rivermont, there's an assumption that I live in the hood. Well, some hood *ish* can take place from time to time but, overall, it's pretty safe for those who reside here. Residents know who engages in illegal activity and they don't care to mess with those who aren't a part of that lifestyle. I've been here for a few years now and my circle is pretty tight. We have our issues here and there but, for the most part, I stay with the same small crew.

We hear about the girls who are freaking all the boys and chime in about recent fights. Everyone knows everyone and when something goes down, the word is out in little to no time. It's summer time and the cookouts are in full swing: when evening comes, you can smell the aroma of burgers on the grill, hear card players yelling about who's cheating and beer cans make an appearance.

Cookouts are a good time: the adults are happy, music fills the air and the smell of grilled food makes you want to crash the party for a plate. Most times these events are carefree with no drama or police needed. The kids get to play out late because the parents are entertained; if you're lucky they get to dancing. I love these moments and I wish they came more often. In these times, I'm proud to say I'm from Rivermont and reppin' my neighborhood feels damn good.

Best Friend
By Brandy

I've been so hard on you because I'm afraid someone will take advantage of your kindhearted spirit. From the day I entered this world, you were there. We've been playmates, roommates and even enemies at times but, I wouldn't change you being my sister for anything in the world. No one knows me better than you do: you see me at my lowest moments and encourage me; you see me at my highest moments and congratulate me. When I'm uncertain, you empower me.

Sis, you've been my best friend since before I even knew what a best friend was. I believe God knew that I needed a partner to hold me down along this journey and he sent you. People tend to come and go in my life but you've been the one constant from the very beginning. Through all the bad times, when I felt life wouldn't get any better, you would give me some intelligent Donelle response that often went over my head but was centered in love. Although we are often like oil and water, I couldn't imagine a life without you.

Even though you snitched on me from time to time and I was pissed at you for you telling, I understood that you cared about me. During my dark years, I pushed you away and our connection changed but I never doubted that you would be there when I needed you. We have moved onto our separate lives; we don't talk as much but, when we do, it's as if time stood still.

Whenever *Best Friend* plays, I recall a time when we practiced for a family reunion talent show. We had our dance together and our lyrics were rehearsed. Grandma watched us repeatedly go over our steps and listened as we discussed the outfits we'd wear and how we'd style our hair. Back then the song was special but, as the years have passed, the message is stronger and more applicable. I know I can always count on you to have my back despite the argument or distance between us.

My prayer is that God continues to bless me to spend the rest of my life with my twin who is sometimes my best friend, lol. Love you!

Baby I'm For Real (Natural High)
By After 7

It was our first date: we had spent countless hours sharing our lives, desires and future goals over the phone. He felt unique; he wasn't about the street life. He shared my passion for knowledge: we wanted similar things; we grew up in some s--- but we made it to adulthood with enough strength to carve out some peace and happiness.

We were fighters. I found myself staring at him because I couldn't believe this creature existed and wasn't a figment of my imagination. I did my best to stay focused on the conversation but I was often fantasizing in my head, waiting for the dream to soon be over.

He was polished and dressed as if he had prepared for a special evening. His scent had entered my space before we embraced; damn he smelled delicious. We started our evening at a bookstore: he shared some of his favorite authors and I shared mine.

Afterward, we weren't ready for the evening to end; we had spent hours talking but had plenty more to say. We decided to head to the airport park and watch the planes as they passed by. As *After 7* played through his car speakers, he held onto my hand so tightly, staring in my eyes and listening to every word that left my mouth. I couldn't tell you what I was talking about but I felt a different kind of peace, one that I had never experienced before. I knew at that moment that I'd do everything I could to make things work. I was prepared to love him, faults and all, for the rest of my life. We talked about our futures, plans for a better life and, as *After 7* played, my thoughts ventured off into a happy ending that only my heart could conceive.

Can You Stand The Game
By Pastor Troy

Since middle school, we had a connection: something about our zodiac signs made us just mesh. We were cool, real cool; he was short and funny, nothing close to anyone I'd ever been interested in. He was my friend: we talked about him and his love interests and I shared mine. We had commonalities: school sucked, our families were our world, we were stubborn as hell and marched to the beat of our own drums.

We lost contact for a few years after middle school: I found out he got in some trouble and was sent to a juvenile detention center. I wrote him but his comments about me began to change. He was showing a different interest in me but we weren't on the same page. In high school, we sporadically kept in touch; I shared my demons with him and he shared his own. We talked about our significant others; he congratulated me on the birth of my daughter.

Although he was interested, we both decided a friendship was more important than anything sexual. Flash forward a few years: I'm a single mother struggling to make a better life for my daughter. He finds me heartbroken, emotionally drained and bitter. As we embrace, he promises to help me pick up the pieces of my heart and find my happy space.

A budding relationship appears but I know he's caught up in the street life. Love isn't enough to stay around and pray; this time is different. We are starting on different paths: I'm trying to seek out success in education while he's hustling to make a come up from selling drugs. I couldn't do it anymore; I had been down that road before. The last time I gave my heart to someone like that, it ended horribly.

This time, I decided to bow out while my heart was strong enough to handle another goodbye. The night I decided to walk away, Pastor Troy played in the background. The lyrics brought tears to my eyes: he was something special but I couldn't stand the game. I drove down the road with the song on replay and the lyrics etched in my soul; the love permanently written in my book of love.

Boys To Men
By New Edition

I've watched you go from a boy to a man. The journey hasn't been easy because you've experienced many of the same challenges I have. Bruh, no matter the obstacle, you pushed through and were committed to a better life. Even though I see the beard and hear the grown man voice, I'll forever see my baby brother. The baby brother who looked up to me and saw me as his crazy and protective big sister.

Back when dad was gone, I wanted to step in and make things better for you. I knew you missed him and your longing for the connection was much different than mine. You wanted to establish manhood based on his example but life had alternate plans. The beauty is you developed manhood and grew to make us all so very proud.

When you left school and said you weren't going back, I was devastated but you assured me it would be okay. You were right; I was elated to see you finish school and make real boss moves. Each time I watch you as a father to your child, I'm reminded of the man you've become and I'm proud to be your sister. You're the happy medium between your siblings; as chill as one twin but as spitfire as the other.

Little Big Bruh, as time passes I see the evolution in your eyes and seek your wisdom when I'm unsure. We've been thick as thieves from early on; I nurtured you until you no longer needed it. I witnessed your wings develop and struggled to accept when you were ready to fly away (it was time). Luckily, our bond is solid and whenever I need to escape and clear my head, you're a quick text message away.

"Wassup Sis? Come chill for bit; you know I got you!"

Although our roles are sometimes reversed, you still let me be Big Sis and I'm honored to have you as my Little Big Bro! I love you.

Good Girl
By Carrie Underwood

Why are you staying girl? You say you're staying for the kids but he's no good. You hear the chatter in the streets but you refuse to accept it as truth. You spend hours on the phone with me as you tell me how you're going to make the relationship better. You overlook one important fact: the missing/weakest link is him. He's no good but I would never say that to you because you don't want to hear the truth.

We've been friends for so many years and I know that you love him. I understand that you want your family to stay together. You've encountered abuse and blamed yourself for it every time:

> *"It was my fault; I shouldn't have provoked him."*

> *"I knew he was stressed and my nagging only made things worse."*

I've been there as you applied makeup to your face, swearing those bruises came from your clumsiness. I knew the truth; I offered you an escape and believed you would take it. You did for a while; you packed up the kids and ended up at my front door.

I was always the one you could depend on and this time would be no different. We talked about how you were ready for a fresh start and your plans to create a new life. Then time passed: *he's changing,* you said; *he's not the same person* and *he wants his family back.* I cringed from a distance upon your return while understanding that these are the choices you are to make. I heard you pump him up; sharing how hard he had been working to provide for his family.

He's working hard.

He really loves me.

He is a good man.

Never mind his long periods away from home, the unreturned phone calls and the nights you slept alone while waiting. While I listen and try my best to be your support, we both know that you know the truth but aren't quite ready to accept it. So I sit and wait for the day that you will decide that enough is enough. The day you choose your worth over the manufactured fairytale and leave.

Until then, I pray angels watch over you as you go through. In love I remind you that I am always here for you.

Family Reunion
By The O'Jays

She stands before us, her family, and sings a song of praise with her powerful, robust voice. Before she began to sing, there was an incoherent chatter in the room which competed with music from the speakers. I was running along with my Baltimore cousins, attempting to keep up with their conversations (city living was faster than my hometown). When they shared their experiences with crime, often their stories were things I had only heard or seen on television. I love family reunions because my family tends to put me onto the latest songs, fashion trends and sayings.

But all conversations and noise came to an abrupt stop when my Auntie stood before the family. Before she entered into melodious song, she reminded us of the family members who were no longer with us. She talked about how proud her father would be to see all his offspring and her siblings chimed in. I am proud to come from such a diverse group of people and I'm warmed by the connection my grandmother shares with her siblings. Auntie transitioned into her testimony through song; as she sung, those who knew the words sung along. I had heard the song before but not enough to lend my voice to it.

I listened and hummed along while basking in the precious moment of being a member of this family. We aren't perfect and, just like any other family, we have our share of drama. The difference is in the love that we have for one another; it is evident, especially in these moments. I was too young to grasp how precious those times were and lacked the wisdom of how time would soon take many of my loved ones away. But, in that moment, I was full and immensely proud of my heritage.

Throughout the building, while my Auntie sung as if the Lord stood before her, I saw the various shades of brown that made up my family. I pondered over our differences; the unique experiences that we shared, interwoven by the fabric of love. As I reflect on those times, I think about how lucky I am to spend each year with my family at our reunions.

Crossroads
By Bone Thugs N Harmony

He was taken before he had an opportunity to enjoy adulthood. I was very young when someone took his life. I didn't understand back then how definitive death was. I didn't understand that when my father said he was gone, that meant he was gone forever. I'm not sure if I had ever seen a body in a casket before his death but the memory stayed with me for many years to come.

My cousin was a cool dude and, although he was much older than me, he would take time to play with me before leaving to hang with the adults. I thought he was a rockstar because his extrovert personality gained him countless connections. When we were in town, people would shout "Hey" and treat him like he was a local celebrity. His charismatic approach helped most people feel comfortable. I paid close attention to his dress, his swag and the way he owned a space when he entered the room.

Dad was partial to him because he was very respectful and he knew that fun wasn't far behind whenever he came around. I was still in elementary school whenever "Cuz" stopped by; Dad would be chill, music might be played or the cards came out. Nevertheless, whenever "Cuz" was in town, the good times were in full effect.

Perhaps that is why, the day I learned of his death, I couldn't grasp the magnitude of the pain that followed. My Aunt was devastated and my family struggled to accept that he was taken far too soon. Throughout my childhood, I thought about him and the life he missed out on. As I reached adulthood, I imagined what his kids would look like if he had lived long enough to have any.

I wondered what career path "Cuz" would have chosen and how much more fun we could have shared along the way.

The beauty of life and death is, when my time comes, I'll get to see him again one day. I smile as I think about how much he is enjoying his time with those who have crossed over. I vow to do my best to enjoy my time here and add a little of his fun along the way. Cuz, until we meet again!

Lean On Me
By Bill Withers

We've been friends for so long that now you're extended family. Life sometimes leaves you thinking that you're doing this all alone but, remember, you can always reach out to me. Please don't allow pride to keep you from gaining a listening ear or a comfortable place to rest your head.

Remember back when times were hard and I called you with a request? You know, when he didn't do his part and I had to find another place to stay? My family didn't understand and I couldn't bring myself to ask them for help so, I called and asked: *"Can I crash on your sofa until my apartment is ready?"* What was your response? *"Sure."* Just like that: no questions asked, no lectures or I-told-you-so; you simply reminded me that things would get better. You kicked your kids out of their bed to give me a space to lick my wounds and recover. I'll never forget what you did for me that day.

So now that you stand in need, don't afraid or wonder if it is okay to ask me for help? Let me reassure you: we are forever connected and I'll do whatever I can to support you. You've made my journey easier by listening to my rants, reminding me of my accomplishments when all I could see was my failures and you did all that by simply being there. You were born an only child but God added a younger sister to your plate. I admire how you mother your children and conquer life all while being your fly self.

You are a warrior in every essence of the word and, sometimes while in battle, you need an ally (we all do). I will be that for you. When you feel all alone, call me;

when you need someone to be there, I am your girl. Our paths connected over 10 years ago and, at first hello, I knew we would be friends. Since that time, we have evolved to family and I can't wait to see what the future holds.

No matter what it is, if I got it, it's yours for the taking. You can always lean and depend on me!

I Wanna Dance With Somebody (Who Loves Me)
By Whitney Houston

My grandmother and siblings are in the other room so I sneak and put on Grandma's red pumps and pretend to be her before I got caught. Whitney's video came on just in time for me to dance: I put on her shoes although I could barely stand in them. I positioned my feet so they didn't fall off as I stood in front of her closet mirror and did my best version of Whitney.

I envisioned being at the club and dancing in a beautiful red dress, red lipstick and red shoes like the ones that I could barely wear. The electric groove of the song helped me to sway and shake like I saw the dancers do on TV. I was too young to understand the message behind the lyrics but I felt the pure pleasure as I danced to the beat.

Adulthood seemed like something so cool and I couldn't wait to move past childhood to dance with someone who loved me. As I moved in circles and sung along, my grandmother made her way to the room to see what I was doing. I dashed to her bed, hiding the shoes back under her table. She looked at me and, I could tell from the look on her face that, she wasn't buying that I was in her bed watching the video.

"What you doing?" I responded with an innocent "nothing". Knowing it was a lie, I looked away to avoid her reading the truth on my face. Just in time, Whitney saved me with her chorus. My sister, who stood behind her, had no idea what fun I just experienced while in granny's shoes. I smiled a big smile while singing along to the chorus. I still saw red pumps and dancing in my future but without Grandma around. Lord knows she would have got my butt for playing in her "expensive shoes".

Don't Want To Be A Fool
By Luther Vandross

I refuse to be hurt again. I've given my heart away too many times and each time has left me more broken and devastated. Not this time! *You're different*, you say; you *won't put me through those same changes.* You want a chance to *prove to me that love can be different.* Well sorry, I am not gambling with my heart anymore.

The last time I was hurt, it broke me down to my core; it took years to rebuild myself from the pain of loving and leaving. I promised myself during those nights when liquor bottles filled my nightstand, that no one would fool me again. I promised myself that I'd spend the rest of my days guarding my heart from liars, cheaters, deceivers and immature idiots who didn't deserve the love that I had to give. I don't want to chance ever returning to that dark space again.

You stand before me with sadness in your eyes, begging for a chance, trying to assure me that, this time, I will be treasured to make up for what others took for granted. But I am simply not ready; I can't even tell you if and when I will ever be ready. Love is a tricky thing: it can make you feel like you're flying in the sky and make you plead for the pain to go away. I've ridden on the rollercoaster of love and, although I miss that incredible high, I cannot survive another low nor be broken ever again.

I decided a long time ago to focus on those things that cause the least amount of pain. I decided to put my energy into my children, to grow my professional platform and focus on things that preserve my sanity. Love has the power to leave me unbalanced and crazy.

Love had me giving more of myself without requiring for the receiver to reciprocate. I don't know that healthy love you talk about or promise to give me.

I am not healed enough to open my heart to another. I am not healed enough to trust that your words or deeds will be any different from all the others. My mind knows that you are not "them" and that, one day, I have to move on. But today is not that day; I am not ready for the leap of faith required to receive your love or trust and I refuse to ask you to stay around for an uncertain possibility. So instead, I encourage you to go out and find someone willing to risk it all and give you the love that you desire.

I Still Say Thank You
By Smokie Norful

I'm in my thirties now and, so far, I have had a full life. Lord willing, I will have many more years to create additional unforgettable memories. When I thought my life was over, I begged you for more time. I prayed that, despite the time I wasted, you would bless me with more time. Lord, thank you for granting my prayer.

Since the heart attack, I've been on a mission to use any day that you grant me to fulfill my purpose. This journey hasn't been easy, and now I face more obstacles than before, but I thank you for it all. Being forced to live by faith alone and walk in my truth, revealed the strength and power I never knew I had.

When fear and pride raise their ugly head, I am reminded of the night that I poured my heart out to you and vowed to live differently. As a result, I gave no room to those limiting beliefs designed to darken my path. My testimony is a reflection of how God can take anyone and use them for his greater good. You took a little girl who suffered from low self-esteem, who didn't have any earthly idea how she fit into this world and blessed her to raise two miracles. You've walked me through despair and held my hand when I couldn't call or depend on anyone else.

What a great injustice I would serve if I did not acknowledge how you ordered my steps and placed angels along my way. I acknowledge that nothing has happened in my life without it being ordered or permitted. The abuse, the sickness and all the sleepless nights, developed a warrior in me that is unstoppable. I may never grasp the magnitude of all the blessings that you've provided me, in spite of me. You didn't have to do it but you opened doors and allowed me another chance to get things right.

Another chance to appreciate the time I have here and to cherish those that I love. To inspire the masses to live and boldly walk in their truth. To step out on faith and trust that, with hard work and dedication, all things are possible.

So for my life, my mother, father, sister, brother, children, grandparents and my entire family and friends, God I simply say, Thank You!

As I close . . .

This book of short stories has uncovered so many memories. It took me years to develop them into stories and even longer to reach a place where I was comfortable enough to share them with the universe. I can't walk away from this book without acknowledging some of the people who have shaped the Danielle who stands before you, proudly sharing my story and imparting wisdom to anyone who will listen.

I wouldn't be the woman I am without those who helped me along the way; I spoke of many of them in my stories. God has allowed me to share this journey with parents and grandparents who sowed into me when I was a challenge to love. My grandmother would often say, "I pray I live to see you be successful!" Well, Grandma, every day I have the opportunity to walk this earth and empower another, your prayer has been answered.

I don't have all the financial success I desire but I am rich in all the things that money cannot buy. Nothing on this earth is more important to me than the connections that I share with my family. I love you Mom and Dad. Grandma Linda and Grandma & Grandpa Jackson, I want you to know that I have the privilege to spend the rest of my life building a legacy because of the foundation you sowed. The three of you have been a staple in my life and our connection will outlive us all. This book is dedicated to you!

I pray that years from now, someone reads these stories and is blessed by the precious moments we have shared.

Brown Eyes, thank you for your love and dedication. I am working on putting into words how your love helped transform my life. (I see a sequel in my future...) Caleb, I'm honored to be your other mother and I love you as if I birthed you myself. I look forward to see your gifts flourish into manhood.

As I say farewell, my final message is to my children, Arianna and Amari. Always remember that, regardless of what life brings, whether joy or pain, God is always right there with you. Dream BIG, Stay Determined, & be a WARRIOR like your mother!

Love & Blessings,

Danielle Boose-McDowell

A special thanks to Alesha Brown, of Alesha Brown LLC, for helping me edit this book. If you need editing services or help writing your book, please contact her at:

TheJoyGuru.net   OR   aleshabrownllc@gmail.com

www.ingramcontent.com/pod-product-compliance
Lightning Source LLC
Chambersburg PA
CBHW032036090426
42741CB00006B/839